THE SUBLIME
and the
Ridiculous

A poetic meander through life

Ashley Burgoyne
&
Melissa Collin

Front and back cover by Melissa Collin

All illustrations by Melissa Collin

The authors would like to thank the editors of the following
publications, in which some of these poems first appeared: *Ambit*;
Birdsuit; Ink, Sweat & Tears and various competition anthologies from
the Norwich Writers' Circle Open Poetry Competition.

ashleyburgoyne.wixsite.com/writerandcomposer
seaislighterthanthesky.blogspot.co.uk

For Mum & Dad ~ A.B.

For Mum,
and for those who people these
poems ~ M.C.

THE AUTHORS

Ashley Burgoyne is a writer, composer and classical guitar teacher. Originally from Luton; which means that he has remained loyal to the often-torturous ordeal of supporting The Hatters, he has lived in North Norfolk for thirty years.
He is married with two children and a daft cat!

A Northerner in exile, **Melissa Collin** has worked in publishing and education since moving to Norfolk twenty-five years ago. She lives in artistic chaos on the North Norfolk coast with her husband and teenage daughter.
She also has a daft cat!

CONTENTS

In the Beginning…

A Seed

To plant a seed
Gives life a chance
If I plant half a seed
Do I only have half a chance?
To dance
On the moon
'til half past noon
And sip tea
By the sea
Whilst the ape
In the tree
Looks down on
Natural selection
And thinks
He's better
As I'm the one
Getting wetter
As the sea
Reaches my knee
As I pour
Another cup
Of tea
From a pot
Bought
From a market
In Harrow
On it
A drawing
Of a sparrow
Drinking tea
Shouldn't he
Be eating a seed?
If he did
He would have a chance
To succeed
Unless
It was only
Half a seed

Mid-winter

It comes down to this –
a flattened Atlas, a relief map.
Neon-green are the
mountains and high ground;
their contours delineated.
They ooze like mercury.

You are too tiny to be
seen from above water,
so they send in a submersible
to look for your outline;
the black, powerful beat of your heart,
flicking in double-time in the dark.

Faces are set. They have seen
the hot, heart-bound flowerings
that stink of metal.
Magma rising to the surface,
leaving a dead, still core; cooling.
There is nothing here to see

except stillness. Outside it is
mid-winter, and for the first time
I know that I am not God.
You will be with me for one more day,
like a secret I no longer wish to keep.

Porthmeor

From our gull-harassed house
we can almost see Newfoundland.
Across a whole half-globe of
ice-green Atlantic, whales
nose the deep soundings.

Your sonar; quick dull thuds,
echoes across the depths.
You are as unknown and unseen
as the frosted wastes of the Arctic,
as the North Atlantic Drift

and yet we search horizons
through sea mist and spray.
Nightly, your eddies swirl,
mercury-thick, against the
granite full-stop of the cliffs.

Birth

It's funny when we are young
we enter this world near a bum.

Is that significant?

Spring

Seems to promise so much
with its thin, peeled-skin leaves unfolding
like the new wet wings of butterflies.
We are still here by the fast river
where shark-eyed pike trawl the deep swims
and the only embryos are the
weighted bald heads of snowdrops.
The birds think they are naming the world anew
and slicks of ducks are caught in the eddies;
thrown along the deep green melt-water.

Childhood…

The Brazen-ness of Bones

How could it be so brazen, this thing
that took an age and a crying to be here?
The first one; pearlescent in its pink bed,
has always been brazen, with its

white soldier cousins, milk-soft and
upstanding in their fallible regiment.
I nurtured them, these tyrants, feeding
them ambrosia and bones and blessed air

and they came in their legions, each one
with a fever and a raw, dank breath from
an earthy cave. The cathedral-vaulted nave
welcomed them for a week, a month, a year;

herringboned redly around them and choired
by a thin, reedy whine. Now it stands
on the red cliff's edge, its successor
making a coup; bloodless and cold.

Grandma

Hold grandma's hand to cross the road.
Hold grandma's hand, you have been told.
When mummy's not here, grandma is near.
Too bloody near when she's holding your hand.

Let's go to the park, let's feed that duck.
Let me play on the swing, I fancy an ice cream.
No, home for a sandwich and some battenburg.
The thing with grandmas, have you heard is

With food round your mouth out comes the hanky.
With relish she spits on that, there, hanky.
Under protest she rubs it over your face.
And at night, in my prayers, I say to God, for grandmas, I thank thee.

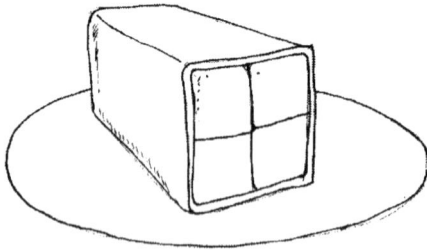

Seals

Out there, where the sea trembles like mercury
under the cooling violet of the dusk sky,
seals raise their boulder-shiny heads
and doggy-paddle, cutting a thin wake
through the smooth water.

On the clacking hillock of flints
our unsure feet meet the body of a seal,
eyeless, where the gulls have been at him.
Fur salt-thickened and stuck in stiff folds.
Leathery hands clasp the pebbles.

Near him is the perfect skeleton of a fish;
the memory of the chase, and now
the sea wants him back. Next high tide
he will be keel-hauled with fish; picked clean.
Sleek silhouette rolled to coral.

Friends

'Is he coming out to play?'
Darren would say
to my mother at the door.
'Are you going out?'
my mum would shout.
She needn't say any more.

'Hang on, I'm coming!'

'Now don't be long
and don't go far,
it's nearly time for tea.'
I get out my bike
and walk it down the drive.
His was green, mine was red,
it was great to be alive.

Down the park, over the grass,
nipping through the gears.
Do you remember the lever
was in between your knees?
That was really weird.

And then my chain would come off.

We'd stop off at Richard's and see if he was in.
But he was nearly always at his dad's.
Why wasn't his mum with him as well?
She could do with cheering up,
she always looked so sad.

Then round our racetrack,
Darren would win
because my chain would be dragging along the floor.
Then home for tea and I'd wait again
for Darren to come to the door.

Football

Pass
I'm in space
Pass
I've got the pace
Knock it through
Simon
I'm on, I'm on!
No
He gave it to Fred
Who controlled it
With his head
Then fell on his face
Due to a lack of space.
Space I have
And pace
But that's not all,
I also never seem
To have the ball!

Heights

The church is caught,
gaunt; a documentary item
in the cruel round of memory.
Silhouetted against the moor's cloak
its dead bell peals unheard
across acres of peat-dark fields.

The moor yields up its secrets rarely;
and this one it guards.

Pews gather dust in the stone-dank
guts of the building. The moor winds
creak through its gaps: a galleon
on the shoulder of the hill.

Our devotions are now given to more obscure gods.
Sheets of slate blind the windows.

Three houses are shuttered closely.
At night we hide our fires.
From the valley no light can be seen
as the dead streak like lightning
through the razor grasses of the heath.

God

Dear God,
What's your 'phone number?
I tried the operator, but she didn't know.
She said it was misplaced when they last changed the code.
I tried to fax and e-mail ya,
but both of them were also a failure.
So, I thought and pondered on what might not fail
and at last I remembered the old Royal Mail.

So, here I am with pen and ink
and I really am trying to think
about how to ask in this letter
if, dear God, you can make my gran better.
You see she's ever so old and her face has gone pale,
her legs are weak and her body frail.
When she last went to church she said a prayer for me,
so, in turn I'm writing this letter for my granny.

I pray, dear God, that you in heaven
can help my granny reach 87.
The Father, the Son and the Holy Ghost,
Amen.

P.S. What's your address? I'll try 'God. FREEPOST.'

FAIRY TALES

Woven In

I.
Once my head was off
a new house was needed,
as though the stones had blood
so soaked into their porous,
gritty hearts that no water
could wash them clean.

The pond fills slowly;
it rains so rarely. The weed
waits, with the one shark-eyed
pike in the shallows. Men
build slowly, stone by stone,
until the roof shines in its

dull, red brilliance;
fakey turrets crowing in
fat glory over the dry moat.
They are a bold bunch.
The wainscoting is shined
to a rich red sheen.

II.
In another country women stitch,
between sharp white wings,
at raw canvas; threads coloured
with saffron, spinach, beetles' blood
shape face after face.
I get myself in there, somehow,

with some sleight of hand.
They said I was a witch.
At night I step down, taking with me
my newly stitched head that is wiser
than my old one. Corporeally,
I walk their halls, feet ringing.

Joan of Arc

I.

They begin;
small whispers that round my ears.
See: I am doing it myself,
turning in my vision,
turning it in to the mad orbit of days.
They begin, with their sleight of hand,
thrusting me into tight corners of space.
I cannot be alone with these things,
these thoughts that spill into each musty corner.

I am silent and unmistakably sheened,
with my mouth lapsed open.
They speak, in vast curls of roundness,
in mixed lyricism.
My ears are buzzing with the feel of them
and the ache of the flames crawling higher.
They are oozing through the cracks in my door,
their oily presence.

And so I cut off all my hair
and fit myself for battle,
naked and glowing beneath
the looped casings of my armour.
No longer silent I am speaking in tongues,
loosing my mouth with good wine
like the soldiers do.
I spiral higher; let battle commence.

II.

They gather the dead rushes into crude bundles,
tying the ends with hair and spun thread.
The pyres are built with care, the songs
of the builders drifting over to where
I kneel in my shift; more girl than warrior.
My eyes are raised to my own sacrifice
as they douse the pyres with oils and perfumes.
The mouths of the priests are wet with mead.
My own starved lips mouth my endings.

They lift me like a prize, these glazed men,
and call upon their faiths to carry me away
on their burning fronds; their conscience.
The flames lick my thighs. My own scent hangs
and cloys and it scares me, oh it scares me
when I see how men fall and flay themselves
at my feet like penitent saints or cracked gods.

Rapunzel

From my tower I can see
the tops of the far trees.
I can see them coming,
one by one,
these half-dead men.
Curiosity fires my blood
and I burn like a beacon
in my high room.

Sometimes they come in twos
and lie in wait,
avoiding each others' eyes.
Rapunzel, they say,
let down your hair.
And so I do.
I do as my senses bid.

My charmed locks fall,
grazing their faces and they climb.
Each one more trusting than the last;
each one more sure.
My daring grows,
drawing them in
with octopus feelers.

Christmas Day

Christmas Day is a strange time.
You get up at 6, instead of at 9.
Then you hand round lots of presents; that's nice.
But not many people say 'Happy Birthday, Jesus Christ.'

At 1 o'clock you get your turkey din
and there's absolutely no chance of staying thin.
Then at 3 on comes The Queen.
She always starts by saying 'What a good year it's been.'

By 3.15 everyone's having a nap.
Which is probably wise 'coz the T.V.'s crap.
At 6 it's time for a piece of Christmas cake
and that's probably all your stomach can take.

By 8 the black and white film is on Channel 4
and everyone says 'I've seen this before.'
Of course you have, it's the same every year.
Just like Christmas and the New Year.

Growing up…

When you are young you should be seen and not heard.
You must therefore resemble a bill-less bird!
Flying around without a voice;
but then as a child, you see, you have no choice.

When you're in company you must remain quite still.
You are allowed to breathe though, so as to avoid becoming ill.
In the silence you feel that even a squeak would be nice;
but you're a child, my dear, leave the squeaking to the mice!

But now you're 18 you can be heard and seen;
that means you've now got something in common with the Queen.
She parties, you know, all night long;
but remember,
now you're an adult,
it's your responsibility,
in case of accidents,
to always keep clean undies on!

Questions

Can a man
make a plan
that will decipher a woman?

Can a woman
read a map
so that we avoid a mishap?

Can a boy
find a toy
that he will not destroy?

Can a girl
not get in a whirl
if her hair starts to curl?

Can mankind
find
a way to be kind
to everyone regardless of what goes on in their individual mind?

What the Fruit Becomes

Each year I do as my mother did
and hers before her; tending each
soft bud in its green carapace.
The birds take their few, calling.

The summer does its work,
swelling the flesh, each fruit nurtured.
The neighbours look askance,
always, at my empty belly

and my heart full of song.
Then, sweet juice calms their children's
fevers, soothes away troubles.
A miracle; but the whispers begin.

In the orchard they cut apple wood.
Its sweetness carries always on the air,
oblivious to its destiny. They plan;
the wood is stacked for years, tinder-dry.

I know, when they come for me,
that it will catch at the first spark.

Bat versus Cat

A small drop of light
Is a fright
For a bat
'Coz a cat
Would then see
The bat
For its tea.

But,
Would the cat
Catch the bat
As it flies
Way up high?

Unless,
The cat
Was in a tree
Pre-empting that its tea
Would fly by he…

But,
Cat's eyes are good
At night as well
So the bat
Needs to be careful
And fly
Like a bat out of hell!

Shopping

Shops are so hot.
Do you find shops hot?
Shops are always hot.
Whether the weather outside is or is not.

Fruit and Veg

Fruit and veg are extremely rude.
For such kinds of healthy food.
Carrots, melons and cucumbers
and we mustn't forget bananas.

Moral: don't hang around these veggies in the nude.

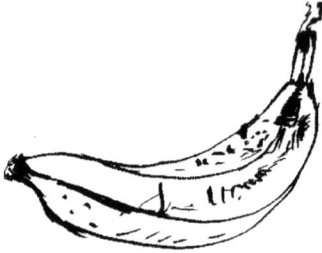

All there is to say about scarlet

He has fenced this place in;
walled it with scented shrubs
to hide the limestone walls
that are as tall as three of me.

The birds return each year;
little bright finches that swoop
in their crazy drunken flights
from branch to branch,

dizzy on the sweet buds.
The earth says so much
about us; our likes, our dislikes.
Each year we insert our own desires

that it takes or rejects with its own
unclouded judgment. The shoots,
that with scant care urge upwards,
or not, as they choose.

Then, one day, a scarlet flower
that says all there is to say about scarlet;
how it swells from red to orange.
The bees agree, as they take

their pollen-dusted bellies
from flower to flower.
There is no stopping it as it sails
Giantwards on its never-ending stalk.

The small green bud swells at its heart.

Charity

Charity is nice.
It can buy shoes for mice.
But only for ones in the third world.
Mice in my street still have cold feet.

Charity II

They say that charity should start at home.
So, I've bought a new fishing rod
for my garden gnome.

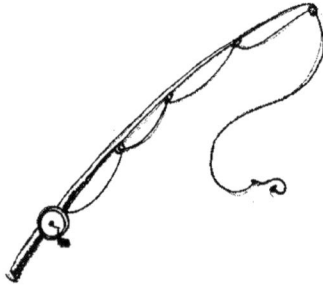

Things Unseen

When all is said and done
You cannot see your bum
Unless you use a mirror
But that would just be weird
Wouldn't it?

Wouldn't you like to know
What your elbow
Looked like?
Probably not a fright
Like your bum
Might be

Wouldn't you like to look at yourself
Looking in another direction?
'Coz when you look
You look, you see
But the reflection is always
Looking back, at me

Wouldn't one's soul
Be good to see
I do mean soul and not sole
'Coz one's sole can be seen
Depending on flexibility

A Deceit of Lapwings

A call goes out – of fog and smoldering.
On the air is a sound of vibration – proximity
Radiates static. The air is alive with it.
The low-slung sun cuts cloud banks

Across mathematical furrows powdered
With morning luminescence.
All forward motion is alive with possibilities.
A bell tower glowers from the sump
Of a field – richly umber and watered with sky.

Telepathically our wires crackle and sag.
A feather is light with it. The bird's
Weightless undersides aerodynamically
Lift with song – with the Morse that
Beats winglessly towards you.

Moving on…

Chair

If a chair
Is there
It seems only fair
To sit
Upon the seat
And eat
The meat
Sandwich
Which
Was made
With care

Two slices
Buttered
No words
Were uttered
As it was spread
Upon the bread
And ham
From a can
Was placed within
Relieved from the tin
To see out its days
Covered in mayonnaise

A bite
Might
Not reach the ham
For the crust is thick
This sandwich
Is a brick
With butter
For cement
It's meant to be nice
I'll ask the mice
Who under the chair
Look up and stare

A crumb may fall
Only small
But the white beast
By my feet
Will see it as a feast
To eat
And gnaw
Whilst sat on the floor
Which seems unfair
When I'm on the chair

Holidays

Sitting in a deckchair, on the sand.
Lolly or a choc-ice in your hand.
Trousers rolled right up to the knee.
Pouring from your flask yet another cup of tea.
Knotted hanky sat upon your head,
'Coz this is Skeggy, you know, not the Med!
The sun is yet to be seen
as you doze off and fall in to a dream.
You wake with a start,
a pounding in your heart,
with the sea around your feet
splashing up and dampening your seat.
You stand up and cry
'Send for the R.N.L.I.!'

It's ok, it's alright,
it's just a minor fright.
You retreat, up the beach, a bit further back,
sit back down and take another nap.

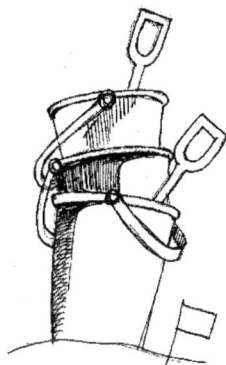

Curlew Cry

The cry of the curlew, where
sea rises faster than a man can walk.
Fog laps the damp, the suck
of salt-fattened mud
on boots and dogs and sea birds.

Dogs seem to surf the marsh,
while men walk their
leaden-footed oily gait in mud
that will embalm them to leather.
Mud swallows men whole.

Wrecked boats settle with
the lowering tides as the wind
clanks through the masts; plovers
whistle from the beds of thrift.
This is the time for skeletons of ships
and bones of men to wash up.

Where Only Giants Can See

The tide rises volcanically through the land,
fattening the mud on salt and air.
Its low-wattage hum works our feet.
Air pushes back on vapour

that threads and waters in the laden sky.
The water strains its meniscus
as birds lift their feet on the updraft.
Men float on ribs of willow and reed.

Shells and stones are honed to sand.
White sails beat where only giants can see,
beyond the stretched, tight horizon.
We are small as gulls, we are

salt and bones and white feathers.

FOUND POEMS

This is a series of 'found' poems composed using an app that scrambles Facebook posts. I have taken the everyday things that I say, and words that occur in other poets' work that I post, and created a new space for them to exist in. I've found this interesting as an exercise in using social media as a tool in what is still seen as a more traditional art form. And to see which words I use a lot. There is plenty of love, sea and weather here....

I.
When we are speaking
Your mouth mirrors the light,
Like rain and soft twilights.

This day cannot stand the constant
Howlings of wind. Nor can the trees,
Or urgent love.

I am more used to my sadness than you are.
The night brings another rose
And eyes the colour of pines.

II.
You meet the weather coming the other way.
I suffer the air.

It is more than love; this fiery kiss,
This animal sunset.

Your stark pupils tell of the hawk's violence,
The hare's blood. The bones at the strandline.

III.
Sea; let me stop now:
The solitude, and this weather.
I've begged to be too much better
Than I seemed; dangerously.

Only the hopeless prayers are left.
You balance your lashes, trying
And failing, to leave everything behind.
Mostly rooks in your shut mouth.

I watch as my words become strained
At your pace. Our rendition of love,
Vast and grey, yearns silently over the house.
You are choral; gregarious at the least.

This more than qualifies me your sweetness.

IV.
You come now and then
Bringing your face before you.
I eat what little you give me.
My smallness grows.

In the woods, where we settle,
Nobody knows us.
We play at love.

Foxes gnaw at my grown nails.

V.
I will know tomorrow if it has been too long.
Hunger makes me sharp; it is my version of wildness.

The moon keeps the men in her wake
From their feral yowlings.
My meanings are blurred.
Yours are more pure.

Your eyes are fine, like mist and clarity.
I eat from them gladly.

VI.
I love with the punctuality of a rainstorm,
Watching your eye's dismay. Oh, but the song
On the sunny beach, made up as you walked

By the rims of anguish. Thinking
I'd go into an endless ecstasy for your boozing stride.

I wait to explain to his face in a photograph.
The others stand still around. I'd hold all the sea;
A snake coiled in the history of forever.
Love – the lungs stretch their intricate wings.

Memories of the evening;
The weft of my lifelong ailment,
The length of our lightening.
A wind still hauls on them

Held in by the blackbirds.

VII.
Today I leave the house for the others.
Lovely things tear my eyes,
But they bleed through the weather – through the sea.

I love the eyes of these stubborn hedges –
No more yours.
What kind of green blood
Swam to your good wishes?

Love and Work...

Daydreaming

Scramble, go, around the bend,
over the jump, back again.
On my bike, as fast as I can.
On this machine I'm the main man.

Boil, my head, whilst at work.
The children scream, my brain hurts.
They talk and shout, never stop,
my head aches and feels so hot.

Fry, in the sun, on the beach.
An ice-cream just within reach.
On a stripy deckchair
without any sort of care.

Poach, that fish, run and hide.
Think up now some sort of lie,
'I caught it down the local stream.'
'A huge salmon? In your dreams!'

'No eggs today,' 'I beg your pardon?'
'"Scrambled, boiled, fried or poached," you asked.'
'Did I? I did, yes, so none today.
Sorry about that, I was miles away!'

It Seemed to Rain

It seemed to rain then – always
the aftertaste of the night before and you,
with your stone saint's face, pale and
Arctic-eyed, waiting for me to break.

Your beauty betrays you – there is
scant kindness in your arsenal, no pity
for the battle-scarred as you stare: your
iron composure. My shoes soak water

as I stand, clown-like, dishevelled by your
gaze, your steady, bore-hole gaze that
makes me naked and stupid. Inconsequential
strata washed away by the relentless force

of your scrutiny. The wide park soaks its
muddy face in rain and faltering birdsong.
This madness says you have the power to
stop the Earth and ease it from its axis.

To Plot a Riot

To plot
A riot
Would take a lot
Of organising
A hot
Bed
Of feeling
Would be rising
During
The organising
And imagine the filing

Position
Position
Map
Position
The precision
Of the mission
No sign
Of commission
For the vision
And the decision
Would be yours
Pause

The thought
Of it
The reward
Of it
Getting caught
For it
I must think more
About
It

Now
No riot
I don't
Wanna try it
Maybe
I'll stick
To some
Kinda diet

Commuting

Sitting on a train with my ear to the seat
Getting red with the heat
Is my ear on the seat
But not as red as the other
Being tortured by a fella
On his phone

It has a microphone
His phone
Although he thinks it's a megaphone
As he tells his missus
Of his boring trip
With no fun at all he would sigh
As he looks at the hand of his PA
On his thigh

Why lie
So loud
Why act
So proud
Does he think he can because we're sat
In first class?
I would so like to shove
That phone up his ass

The Frog Princess

This heart pounds and mocks.
I pull on my frog-skin gear
and wish for someone to turn me
into a princess.
Following sluttish nights
the aftershock leeches like
a sick thing.
The payback.

I open my eyes to a
newly sullied world.
I think this is the answer
but after the pretty boy's
kisses I am still a frog.

Siren Song

This oak is my betrayer, carved
in this place; these
dank walls into which
the sea seems to seep.

The ice-green deep Atlantic
punishes itself on the granite,
white spray torn from the waves.
Men are wrung out on the rocks.

What do they worship here,
the silent, shuttered people
and the huge hungry gulls
that harass the spray-wet slates?

There is more to this than the loss
of a sweet-voiced son. I'm done for,
my eyes gull-holed. My face a scar.
There is no help to be had here.

The men removed my face
with the whistling ease of fireside whittlers.
I'm done for, marooned on my pew-end
while my song keens in the rigging.

The Madonna of the Peninsula

I draw up the sea's whiteness, like litmus;
its brilliance outstares me. Tidelessly, its
flat face beats back the hammer blows
of relentless midday that press flat

the seared land. Arctic water, homeopathically
dilute, recedes to another shore that spewed
out our dull grey sand. The scurf is shorn off
by weighted men under wicker creels.

The man who lights my candles has eyes
steel-hard that the light rings soundlessly off.
My heart sings in its white carapace for him,
for him. I am a beacon for the ships at sea

and the hopeless insomniac walkers who
stalk the cliffs, becoming weightless, as
the dull brass plaques are shined to the sun's
brightness; its deadened saltpan stare.

The Thing With Work

The thing with work
Is it can hurt
The body,
The mind,
The soul.

It's supposed to help you
Achieve a goal.
Instead it leaves
Some kind of hole

Where love was
Is now lost.
The price of earning
Comes at a cost.

Balance,
Where family comes first,
Is gone.
When people thirst

For more than they need.
Evidence of this,
Proof of that.
An unending greed.

Some say
Life's a beach.
Not if
You decide to teach.

School

Schools are full of rules,
just like swimming pools.
No running, no jumping (except in P.E.)
and no petting in the shallow end (unless you're in a video in
P.S.H.E.*)

Yes sir, yes sir, thirty times a lesson;
five minutes later the register's done.
In one ear, out of the other;
knowing that the teacher's thinking 'he's not as bright as his brother.'

Let's shout, let's swear, let's show we don't care.
But teachers can't, they just sit and stare
out of the window, endlessly at the clock,
then in comes the head without even a knock.

Scrape go the chairs,
up they all stand,
'Oh, do sit down,' he says;
'I'm not quite that grand.'

But grand he is; a grand more each week
he gets for sitting on his brown swivel seat.
No children in view, just a computer and paper
and an occasional visit from the Chair of Governors; a baker.

So, ring goes the bell and out through the door
run all the children begging for more.
More of the telly, anything that is cool;
if they were Oliver Twist they'd happily ask for more gruel.

But please; no more school.

* Personal, Social and Health Education.

Dreams

(Dedicated to my wife Jenny)

There are things that we see
in the thoughts in our head,
whilst we're wandering the streets
or we're tucked up in bed.

You see we all have dreams
as men, as lads,
to be a great footballer,
just like my dad.

To see our numbers
come up in the lottery
and buy a big house
with enough left for an...... XR3!

To sail the seas
in a yacht made for a king.
In search of mermaids
and that sort of thing.

To keep our own teeth
and eyes and ears.
So as to avoid queueing up
at the doctors for years.

You may dream to be an actor
of stage and screen.
Or marry into royalty,
'God Save The Queen.'

You may wish to be a rock star
like Mick Jagger or like Sting.
But remember that for this one
it might help if you could sing.

But wait a minute.
Come back down to earth.
Sensible dreams now.
Not just merriment and mirth.

I dreamed to be happy.
I dreamed to be healthy.
I dreamed to get married.
To Jenny.

Dreams do come true
if you open the right doors.
With Jenny I have my dream.
Now pause; applause.

Marriage

To marry, is to carry
the weight of two instead of one.
It is a joining that may bring
a daughter or a son
into this world to join the journey
that is there for all mankind.
A journey that we all make
but not many of us find.
We need to see much further,
to understand our life.
To enjoy what we have on Earth,
as a husband and a wife.
For marriage is the deepest love,
its beauty has no end.
Our need for love comes from above
and remains our eternal friend.

Tilling

I work the soil with my own hard hands
while my neighbour, his sky-blue eyes
ringed with granite, stalks the fields
like the elements that close hard fast around me.

The deep furrows in the raw sienna mud
are waterlogged with bits of the sky.
A rook swims across one, then another.
He raises his gun. The shot thuds in my chest.

Birds scatter like thoughts; outwards.
The kickback jolts his shoulder which is,
I know, suede-soft and softly tanned, giving
gently to the touch of my clay-hard hands.

Waiting for Steve McQueen

It's a roll of thunder; a crack – no more.
A jolt that shimmers my coffee.
We sway
as we walk – anyway
it's a talking point,
like pension plans, away
days and the view –
the sun that knocks the breath from me
each time it burns through the blue
air.

We sway as we walk, like aerialists,
as the towers swing in minute metronomic beats.
The jetstream pours from their tops; crystalline.
We are scaling Annapurna as we fetch paperclips
and fax paper. Scaling and highwire-walking.
Then this crack, this jolt. The dull carpet shivers

and smoke puffs through the weave. On CNN
a phoenix has jigsawed its shape: squatting below
us breathing flames and aviation fuel. Panic statics the air.
I see my red shirt, a table cloth, torn curtains

waving on the big screen.
This is a movie, right?
We're waiting for Steve McQueen.

She

Her face looked tired and crumpled
As it nestled in the soft pillow
Lines of pain and anguish
Held fast by the goose down cloud

Rain beating on the window
Did not affect her slumber
As her breast rose and fell
In time to the tick, tick, tick of the old clock

Breathing deep inside her soul
Eyelids twitch, searching for something
A dream perhaps of other times
When we were young and free

A distant call from a rooster
Makes her turn away from me
Her silhouette now rolling
Like the hills we used to walk

Tony's Takewaway (a sonnet)

It seems an inauspicious place for love
to flourish, on this A road strewn with fags;
and flying on the dust-blown wind above,
the butterflies are made from plastic bags.

But here, beneath his flashing neon sign,
the object of my fevered heart's desire;
the only one I need to make all mine
stands serving scraps, my poorly mind afire.

And when his battered hands reach for the salt
And ease the paper gently round each wrap
My mind is freed from thoughts of guilt and fault
And loss and glides above the pigeon crap.

He sets my heart free soaring from its shell.
There's just one thing: if only he could spell.

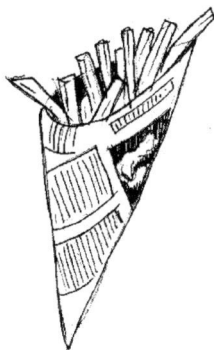

Anniversary

Year upon year.
Child upon child.
Year upon year,
becomes less wild.
But does it?

Boundaries change,
goalposts move.
Brows become furrowed,
that need to be smoothed.
But do they?

We're still wild!
Along with the kids!
The furrows are smiles,
don't keep them hid.

Move on, progress,
change, rise above.
But never forget the person
with whom you fell in love.

Later life…

My Idea of Heaven.

My idea of heaven
is waking up beside you
at 7
or 8, or
even later.

Walking along the misty shore
going for the morning paper.

Hand in hand
across the sand.
With a glint
in our eyes
and a knowing in our heart
that we will never part.

But,
your glint wasn't as clear those days
as I thought it was,
it was merely a haze.

Of lust,
not love.

You never really wanted me,
I can tell.

It doesn't matter what my idea of heaven is.
My heaven is your hell.

Tantamount

That's tantamount to swearing.
That's tantamount, that is.
I couldn't say that, when I were young,
When I were just a kid.

The things they say, and get away with,
That's tantamount I say.
When I were young I wouldn't dare.
Nay, lad, I say nay.

That's tantamount, trust me.
I should know 'n' all.
If you can't say it without swearing
Then you shouldn't bloody say it at all.

Oil Slicks in Siberia

The day you left me, O
oyster's irritant – barely formed,
I watched while
black slicks flooded Siberia.

The world paused, as it does.
My heart was vast and empty
as the Tundra; the iced wind
echoing to the dull thud of

hoof beats; rampaging Cossack dread.
Here; blackness is all there is.
This devastating surge, slick
with oily wetness that
chokes life from everything.

Men probe ice-holes desolately
for dead fish, while sea birds
hunch in their black coats;
old men waiting to die.

Time

Time
Is always constant
Each tick
Is gone
In an instant
Each tock
Enough time
To say
You forgot

Seconds
Into minutes
Into hours
Into days

So much time
Has gone
So much
Forgotten
I'm now so weak
I'm almost
A fortnight

Sun dial
Some denial
Of time
Spent
Cruising
The Nile

That time spent
Is heaven sent
And heaven's scent
Is my lament

Hospitals

'I'm afraid you're not very well, Mr. Jones.
You're going to have to come with us.'
'I feel alright, but if you say so,
I'll nip down the street and catch the next bus.'

'No, we'll get you an ambulance,
it will be here in a minute.
Two men will come
and help you get in it.'

'An ambulance you say, with all the blue lights
and the sirens, what a thrill.
But I'm not too sure about going in to hospital,
it seems to have in it too many people who are ill.'

'My bed's quite comfy and the nurses are nice,
thank you for coming, Doris my dear.
Mr. Carter kept me awake coughing all night,
he may not be with us for long, I fear.'

'I find the bleeping on this machine annoying,
it sounds a bit like a metronome.
Do you think if it plays one note, like Mr. Carter's,
I could also go home?'

Another Year's Corner Has Turned

Our little exile is gale-battered –
the wind's progress from Arctic drifts
over miles of slate grey is halted only
by one ice-age mole-shunt.
A semi-colon. An ellipsis.

The seas drag. They are wreckers here still –
shouldering the door to the snug with
muscles hewn by heft of driftwood;
ironmongery; salt-stung comestibles.
We are one half-mile from the drop
that creeps closer with each winter.

Erosion

This land's invasions are constant.
With each wave the land retreats;
sand met with oily clay, slick
with little waterfalls that bleed
the substance away. Wrecked groynes

rise from the sand like Dunwich bones.
All is anger. Something has it in for
this place. The people run while
their homes are tumbled seawards.
At the foot of the cliff a photograph,

a cracked chamber pot, the bones
of a Yorkshire Terrier. In the summer
we swim, stoically, and sun on the
soft-brown sugar sand, but all the while
there are plots afoot, to take the shacks,

the car park, the lifeboat station. The
lighthouse pulses its semaphore over
the grey clay lips of the land, and
the living and the dead barricade
behind their flint defences.

Harvest Moon

A ship slices the sea from the horizon,
cleanly. This pebble-clacking foreshore
sings in ochres, umbers, straw-wet
sloughed-off layers as dusk falls.

Blackbirds throw their vibratos from
branch to roof and back again
as sky deepens to blood-red over
the sandspit land and cracked wooden hulls.

A salt smell is everywhere. Dew falls
on skin. Silence, then the ripe moon
is neon-bright and low-slung in
the ink-bled, early frosted night.

The Yare at Rockland

A distant V of geese
unwinds its thin skein
eastwards over swaying sedge.
Drawn swiftly, precisely,
thin, wet sepia strokes
blur against the lowering sky.

Smoke also unwinds
from floating houses
cast loose from land.
As land chases its edges,
four horizons ring us.
The land shifts; waterbound.

All our edges are water;
slick, like oil, like pigment
mulled against stone.

The Falling Man

Air is liquid. This surprises me.
I thought – if I'd thought – that
it would be featureless, but still
it parts in its liquidity.

The thinness of the air
stops my breath. If I'd thought,
I would never have done this.
At first, the air was buoyant,

it held me – poised – so I could
see ants in pure, feral panic in
the carefully-ordered checkerboard
streets below me: chaos was never

meant to be here. Air is all I know.
Our relationship is brittle. Essential.

Dad

When you leave this room for the final time
Leave the door ajar,
So that we can remain near you
Our so much-loved Grandpa.

When we stare out to sea
And remember times we had,
We'll think of you with a tear and a smile
Our so much-loved Dad.

We walked through life side by side.
We got through it hand in hand.
We savoured every moment together,
My much-loved husband.

For as long as there is salt in the sea
You'll remain in our minds.
For a finer person in this world
You will never find.

Letting in the Air

After winter, the house has
the air of the sickroom, we are
stagnating in our own sad air.

At work, in the almost Zen
of boredom, we are sickening
one by one. We bear
the odd drunk on the phone;
the hum of the photocopier

and the sick green light in the ladies
that shows every line on our
beat-to-shit faces, like
a child's make-believe.

We gulp for air in the fishbowl light.
But here, in the house, the window
cracked open lets in
the first whisper of spring. The hush
of the brackish, tidal river
and the gentle buzz of songbirds.

26535306R00049

Printed in Poland
by Amazon Fulfillment
Poland Sp. z o.o., Wrocław